To Katy,
Thanks for
love, [signature]

To Kath
with love +
thanks for your support
from
Heather Young
xx

UnHoly Trinity

three new poets

Angel **Readman**
Vali **Stanley**
Heather **Young**

first published 2002 by IRON Press
5 Marden Terrace
Cullercoats
Northumberland
NE30 4PD
England
tel/fax:+44 (0)191 253 1901
Email: seaboy@freenetname.co.uk
web site: www.ironpress.co.uk

ISBN 0 906228 85 9

printed by
Peterson Printers, South Shields

© individual authors 2002
typset in Avant Garde

Cover illustration by Sally Mundy ©
Cover and Book design by
IRON Eye Design @ IRON Press

IRON Press books are distributed by
InPress, Nanholme Mill, Todmorden
OL14 6DA, England
Tel:01706 812338

Contents

Angel **Readman**

- 7 At a Certain Hour
- 8 Mr Wolf
- 10 My Mother was a Sybil
- 12 DC, PVC, Catwoman and Me
- 13 Beside the Tyneside
- 14 Previous Tenant
- 16 Powder Room
- 17 Pretty Face
- 18 What Witches Do
- 20 This House is Not Amityville
- 21 Waking Charlotte
- 23 Morning After Brönte
- 24 Jalapeno's, Extra Cheese
- 25 Belly Dance
- 27 Lasses Night Out
- 29 Mrs Mermaid
- 30 Wake
- 31 What ever Happened to Mary -Mare?
- 32 Romeo's Mistress

Vali **Stanley**

- 37 Morning
- 38 What This Is
- 39 Singing Stones
- 40 Extra
- 41 The Catch
- 42 Artist
- 43 Soft-Top
- 44 Perspective
- 45 Love Bites
- 46 Toadstones
- 47 Lizard
- 48 Discovery
- 49 Ma
- 50 Groupie
- 51 Proverbs
- 52 Mechanic
- 53 Detective
- 54 Beyond The Pale
- 55 Alternatives
- 56 Baggage

Heather **Young**

- 59 Always
- 61 Angel Legs
- 62 Charity Shop Blouse
- 63 Hindsight
- 64 His Wife
- 65 Holiday Snaps
- 66 Lighting Candles
- 67 Muriel and Me and Roy Rogers
- 69 Had They Not Died
- 70 Parcel from Aunt Rose
- 71 Shopping
- 72 Silent Storm
- 74 Sitting Here
- 75 Sonnet XV111
- 76 Sunday School
- 77 Swing
- 78 Still Life: Three Apples
- 79 Turnips
- 81 Blocking The Light

Angel Readman
Powder Room

Angel Readman won a Waterstones prize for her poetry and prose from her MA at The University of Northumbria at Newcastle. In 2000 she won the NWN promise award. She has had work published in several magazines including London Magazine, Envoi, and Mslexia. Previously she has written texts for pubs, posters, and radio commercials.
Also available, *Colours/Colors* , published by Diamond Twig.

At a certain hour

Ask me at the right hour,
and I will spill over
the secret content of shadow.
I will show my favourite light when I elongate.
And we overlap, till it is evening.
By the Eight till Late,

I cannot see the constellations.
Orion, Hunter, his Belt, the Plough
are spilt as glitter over paste.
And the rain is a lacquer on you
Solid, cool,
more silver than a CD moon

Ask, on certain nights the Cosmos
seems so small, I can hardly read the blurred carbon copy.
At times I've almost counted the stars,
accessed every one in a blink.
Ask the sky, I've dusted clouds
wished on ha'penny planets, pocketed a smile.

I've almost touched you.

You eclipse
into neon, and I catch the steamy dusk.
Fog of day, I tread your satellite;
gravity weightless, I float
nameless
as the third man in your space

Mr Wolf

Did I ask for it in mum's cerise heels?,
Beast on the folk's couch, cup and saucer
balanced on paws, says he'll have me back by ten.

Could've been wrong to take a swig,
stroll upstairs to lounge on his bed.
Painted his talons Hot Pink, Vamp
on his picnicking mouth, all the better to feast.
And my, how he melts chocolate
laps my crumb lips with his wet carpet tongue.

Shared Kit Kat, split foil, polite snap.
That mean, Yeah, unpeel my wrapper -
Rake off the good bits, spit out what's left?
I laugh, red to white, as he tickles my feet.
What if I never took off my socks?
Could've ran, good as Goldilocks.

And I dunno if I'm crying, or screaming
or numb.
I think I told him to stop.

Street lamp, rain.
Garnet and amber slide down the glass,
Pulp in his teeth, my juice down his chin.
He spreads me like jam on the sheets,
Chews out sweet nothing crumbs , a mouth full.
And I'd like to think I told him to Fuck off.

But silence is what I'm good at,
I'm all girl. I forget. I forget,
I forget all over the place.
Cottage, to market and home again.
Full moon on my face, I'm were-girl;
Platinum pelt. Rumours rustle
I go all the way.

Peasants' cross their chests when I smear the path.
Warn their hooded daughters. I'm Pig ignorant,
Stiletto trottered. Don't listen…
To the click of me, in my grubby fur collar,
untouch the soft drift of my cape.
Lock up your sons, mind the husband.
Beware, my minty fresh Dracula smile.

Berries blackened too soon.
It's fall. Falling hard in the forest.
Step out cold
from the belly of a wolf.

My Mother was a Sybil

She spoke in many tongues,
Strange prophecies
her mother handed down.
    If the wind changes you'll stay that way.
        Too close will square your vision.
My mother's hands span my face,
collected poppets in sun-bleached frames.
Marrowfat-eyed, she tattooed my irises blue.
    I spy, someone beginning with M...
My mother; snakes in her curlers,
Beseeching a thousand familiars.
    Don't look at me in that tone. I know.
I was conjured, my head in a bottle -
Monochrome, in her 24-inch crystal ball.
Come evening she shed six of her veils,
transformed Mistress, who skated to Russia
Summoned by lovers. Invoking snowstorms
in her sugar bowl; romancing in her kitchen.
A Holka Polka of stars.

Unbewitched morning, satin sheets of tea,
my steaming mother stirred me. Pickled sky,
dry toast, her after-flight hex.
    You'll come to now't with that attitude,
        wind up just like him...
the leech father she divined. I too have sucked
blood from her stone.
    And gone.

My alchemist mother is green cheese
Hecate taunting a man on the moon.
And I unearth her bedroom; sort fossil robes,
Possess the anointed shoes: arched back stilettos
to zodiac Scholl's. Twelve black bags.
Her tarot dished to charity shop,
Charms and mandrake swept to bin.
        Division
of everyone she ever was.   Eclipsed

her spell is broken.
By candlewick, under jewellery box lining,
I find her Voodoo in a toffee tin.
She kept my baby teeth,
    rattled   my old smiles.

DC, PVC, Catwoman and Me

I've bagged Catwoman me.
Well, not exactly. Smaller waist,
bigger arse so it balances out.
Nice bit of gash. Looked now't like Michelle
What's-her-face?, but ye' dinnae look at the dog
when you're strokin' the pussy. Kinky?,
Aye. She was comin' out one of them clubs.

Cheer up love, might never happen.
Tickled her fancy, held her down like Batman
on a good night,`fore that Robin tempted him.
Gev' me one of her nine lives,
 I showed her who held the whip,
Snapped her claws.

I nailed Catwoman me, well not exactly.
Followed my pet down an alley, slinking
black hole I made with a pen knife,
Wet. Shiny as a bin bag. Shut her miaow.
And I won.

Beside the Tyneside

She talks about her favourites,
Bands the movie reminded her of,
sweet and sticky names, Jam, Sugarcubes, Pixies.

"Is Drew Barrymore prettier than me?"

Beside her he talks too loud
in that jacket, maintaining a theory
that Elvis would beat Tom Jones in a fight.

"Even now?", she laughs, "gone zombie?"
He looks at the billboards in her eyes, the ads.
There's a tune in her head she can't name.

The one he does not recognise when she hums.
She asks if she suited the long hair better,
if black is slimming,
if velvet feels better than it looks.

He fancies Chinese, he says, or something.

And I turn off.
Down an alley, towards Monument.
Puzzle
whether crows in the floodlight ever sleep.

Previous Tenant

Doing up a flat I excavate you,
the ground floor tenant I never met.
Scooping cat muck from the kitchen ,
rubber glove-ing all you touched.
My new picture in a grubby frame,
you peer out, the old print underneath.
"How can people live like this?"

Cheap shampoo, school loo roll
make me glad I can only trace you.
Unearthed in an odd brick of Lego,
the fishing net on a bamboo stick you owned.
My locked windows, a view you hold the key to
Empty milk bottles whistling in the wind is your breath.
you're daily set in concrete on the alley wall.

My brush fogs over the bath
your rugby ball sun. Hand drawn
stick smiling crustaceans, jigging fish
and seaweed on dry land. Choking.
Every dado rail, sponged grey/blue
I do over with new straight edges.

"Sad Woman", stubbed under a rug.
On that torn teddy bear frieze in the only bedroom.
A pasted strangeness I can not sand off,
nor pass to white elephant stall
like the toy mouse in a decoupage frame.
Left behind.

With your kettle, and cookie jar.
The mark of you on cringe colour sheets.
The man's belt, and a solitary shoe
in the understairs cupboard , too small for me.
After an era of scouring every crook, I sit
play Wendy House, wait for home to come.

You're gone, cells dusted.
Polished, every yuk you ever touched.
" Not at this address", you drop in
Through my letterbox. Your name on a Sky demand.
Faith Baptist. Were you religious?
A nut? Optimistic? Did you choose
that name for yourself?

You're gone.

Tonight I flicked on the lamp
and you're back. A missed
stain on the switch, rust blood
a current across my palm.

Powder Room

Girl in the queue looks away, so I don't smile.
Last week's laughter, drained.

Whiff of her garments, white as aspirin.
She brushes my arm, drops a tissue,
Scrumpled, her disposable glance,
of an evening.
My fingers are wiped to the sea.

Empty cubicle, the snub of the hand dryer;
Swinging hinge. And her touch where no one sees.
Cold skin on that warm toilet seat.

Pretty Face

The girl wakes in a fever. Might make caramel after,
pour gold into a bowl, or blister on a molten spoon
straight from the pan. Naked Breakfast
rashers of bacon, stretching her morning skin.

Undercover she's pink, silver lined as pilchard.
He did not peck at her flesh. He did not contradict her thighs
to be kind. She's a fondant touch, scooped blubber,
whole acres of sacred cow.
She's something for everyone.

If only she'd loose a little weight… She'd be someone.
Somewhere else now, he's starving on chicken breast,
hankering for Sunday roast, his crème brulee dessert.

No English roses on her doorstep. Pear shape
out of season. But he, loves a woman he can really hold onto.
Do not be sweet. She is not cuddly. She's fat.

FAT, it's a small boned secret, chin wrapped
with rolls of pretty face. On plump pillows, duvet bellied,
the iron bed-head. She's her own Valentine.

Meringue-lit sheets, snow outside-laying.
She's scoffing for two, fills up when he's gone,
Peeling back foil, she flicks red across the room,
scrunches the box. Bites in half his fancy praline heart.

What Witches Do

Last night at the movies, Dawn of the Dead,
He didn't yawn, stretch a sneaky arm round you,
Like he used to, like he's supposed to.
And isn't that why you sit through any of this?

So in the kitchen, the night after,
You find another path to a man's heart.
Bake passion, you make a loaf.
Spread, with the parts of you he did not reach for.

Hubble-bubble. You burn.
Stir your cauldron. Wipe the bread
Wet between your legs.

This is the way the witches ride,
Unbridled.
This is the way to make him care.

Re-heat cold food in your oven.
You knead something. Warm, fresh,
with a crust, not overcooked. Next,
pick off licks of lady-unshaved hair.

This is what witches do.
This is what you do,
utilise what he shed in his comb.

"I've put a speyeell on you...DUM, DUM, DUM , DUM..."

You're a wild woman on the Habitat units,
Gyrating with a bezel Elvis, stalk blue shadows on his moon.
Next, walk into lounge. Supper presented neatly
with a black handled knife.

He asks for more butter, washes you down with stout.
Lost remote control,
You both stare at a documentary
on telly about the Andes, open-mouthed.

Hound-dog grin; Suede tongue.
Lap it up, you're man's best friend
You're the roll to his rock.
Commercial break.

Now and again, you're a couple.
Devouring one another with the sound off.

This house is not Amityville

        but it bleeds. Possessed
by every word he never said. Back of his head,
he's an armchair you try for size when he's not there.
His condiment arm worn slick with overalls,
newsprint, headlines on the velour on his seat.
Van crushing conkers in the drive, so she shushes you
with sports biscuits. There's weather, an update,
the snooker - all the colours he knows without seeing.
Your Easter steps, communion sandals on carpet plastic,
Disastrous first date in that ra-ra skirt.
And his mother-in-law's last cough, witnessed
In the misty casserole of the screen.

This house is not Amityville,   but it clots.
Door handles seizing, drawers full of sighs,
an ache in every creaking stair. Hand me downs,
unhanded, a toddler gone magnolia before you were born.
Braille faced on new anaglypta, your little sister
slides out with cold feet.

These bricks are not haunted
its rooms are papered in thin lidded children.
Not one picture of them without the kids.
Her folded wallet features. Him , high collared,
quiffed in an ice bucket, larger and late.
Piece together,
the day they were wed.

Their home is not a spook house with sirens,
closets popping open with neon skeletons.
If these walls could speak...
They would not. Dumbstruck,
since they said I do.
This place is not Amityville, but it breathes
the things you don't Ever talk about.

Waking Charlotte

I bet Charlotte Bronte would suit my bondage pants.
Zips open, pen in every silver grin.
Even rectory girls bite their nails, she tells me.
As she steps out of the apostle bookcase, I rub for good luck,
She skips over the velvet rope, draws a beard on Bramwell's picture
And complains about his picture of her, that doesn't do her justice.

   Then she's off
    straight to The Black Bull,
       wolf-whistling builders in shorts, chasing crows
                pecking pizza crusts, squawking
the names of toppings as we pass.

Her brother snuck her in once, behind the bar.
Crouched on a stool in his coat, she listened
to men all night long, downed an ale.
But today, with me, she tries everything: Southern
          Comfort, Jack Daniels, Baileys Irish, things
            with paper parasol, Liqueur coffee,
          Two dogs pop,

She tosses and I catch her Chilli nuts.
Her Petite feet float in my buckle boots;
she points to a scar on her brow, that bitch Anne did.
And we wrestle first edition.
Glugging Guinness, she holds a pint in both hands.
Always dainty, a lady, only pissed.

Soon we stagger to the ladies.
A Silhouette of a woman in a short skirt on the sign
she kisses on her way in, clinks a coin and pulls:
Tampons, Handbag-sized hair-spray,
                               forty
breath mints, condoms -
    flavoured Kiwi and lager, shiny bright packets from the

machine.

Then, we're gone.
    Speeding, quill handed on the back of a motorbike.
                        Her neat handwriting fuming bold
clouds.

Charlotte Bronte and her sisters,
always good for a laugh.
Turn it up, she moshes in a crowded club.
Hangs back-stage, to autograph rock star's chests.
                        Spitting at grave
stones, chewing gum, Joy riding.
She's no Jane Austen, she slurs,
High as a steeple,
she dabs streetlight,
Snorts white grains of time

Morning After Brönte

Greasy spoon after-dawn,
unsupported by whalebone,
She rubs thighs weary with clench, reverts
in the queue for Egg and soldiers, a strong cuppa.
Geisha Waltz on caff lino, she skates sanded ice.
Hoarse, faint, her underwear exhibited,
every pore visible, as her face on a gift-shop tea towel.

Slice off the top;
She dips slow toast into my yoke.
Yellow, runny as weather.
My palms on her skull make a bonnet,
as she whispers a whisper,
private as her unborn child. Yawn

She is gone;
a shaved lock of hair behind glass.

Light drizzle lingers over playing fields.
And I cool in a leatherette booth,
Hold her spoon, smooth with fingers.
I read a menu, smash her shell,
to drown all her witches at sea.

Jalapeno's, Extra Cheese

Pull open a Stella,
I ask how many she's been with.
Shake up the can, till all the fizz is gone;
Flat. She answers with question.
" Been what? - Naked? - To sleep? - To the movies?"

"Lovers."

Bends her fingers back, she lists all the lads
she ever kissed. Names like Stee, Andy, Gary,
sink plunging lips, signing their autographs
with sand tongues.
"How did they love me?" she says,
"Let me count the ways...None."

Watching Ricki Lake she slits her wrists;
open mouthed smiles on her skin
her fingers make talk.
"It was just to see the bones moving"
she says, "I'm hungry, starving, bored."

Bound her up in a faded Lou Reed T-shirt,
ordered pizza and hired *American Werewolf in London*.
One eye on special effects, in bed I asked her.
She said she wanted to see what was in her,
see how she worked, before she stopped.

Belly Dance

(for Gus)

Stir fry stall, I drink your flat lager,
crush the carton. Want to go
on the Waltzers, twist with you,   laugh.
Sometimes giddy, sometimes sick,
at the dirty fingernail of a man,
all big top eyes + heart tattoo.
We meander
through hotdog bodies,
stuffed with the sight of cuddly toys.
Tacky,   but I wouldn't mind one,
For you, to win me something pink.
I'm heading towards the distance.
Ferris wheel revolving, like a tassel
on a swollen nipple.

Reggae downpour, beat of a girl.
She's young, thin, undulating,
Caster of spells with smooth hands,
toe rings.   I'm muddy as fake gold,
caught in her candy,
inhale webs of her lotus sky.
The cashmere jumper you loaned me
grows heavy with storm,
long sleeves, lank   as wet hair.

And as you lick your sugar lips,
stare at the bellying girl;
her umbrella spoke lashes,
hips   flat as teapot lids,
I'm without rhythm, bob
a foot behind you,
Arms folded, heavy as toffee,
I'm stuck on your teeth.

What a dancer, she shimmers,
as you unhook my bra.
My breast green as bronze,
your statue.

unHoly trinity

Like two people, eyes set
on a tightrope ,
we're together,
hypnotised   in difference.
Hold on,   to her languid face,
her body,   flickering
adjacent flames.

Lasses Night Out

Pick over cocktails, roast nuts.
salt & vinegar snacks, but No garlic
(You never know your luck)
Sheila tells me my latest
is so much better than the last.
The one they refer to as Lard balls,
unless they're feeling merry, its just bastard.
I'm so lucky she says.

" This one's lush, and, well, thinner."
Sonya agrees, I could do so much better.
They drill for all the gen & Sheila chews my ear off,
subtly yanking knickers from a crack under the table.
"The trouble with men..." Sonya jokes,
I should pass him her way, if I tire of a good thing.
She' tells me how lucky I am.

No decent talent, Sheila's on the pull, she got to try out
the effects of the piercing, down there last month.
"It's the only fucking stud I've got."
Sonya, says, she's saving herself for Robert Carlisle;
then specifies, she only fancies him in *The Full Monty*,
not as Francis Begbie. Someone the spit of him will do.
Ice cubes fizzin' in glasses, the gang make a toast
to me, and my new, all-mod-con fella.
"How did you do it? You're soooooo lucky."

White shirts billow past to the dance floor,
His mates, snorting and woofing at totty at the bar,
Their assessment in stereo. I don't make the grade.
His past rises to the surface of my glass, a chorus line, me on
the end.
I squeal like a needle, stuck on the same groove,
a bit of fluff on a 12" mix.
I'm so lucky.

Sheila rues the banker she chucked cider over.
Steady job, nice car. This is it. Too bad

he made a withdrawal from somebody else's account.

"What a waste! I was enjoying that pint an' all."
Sonya talks spit versus swallow, same as last time
"You jammy bloody bitch."

"We approve", they conclude.
My round - scour out a cigarette,
G&T with a twist, bitter lemon.
I blow bubbles with a striped straw.

Think of the fat man my friends ribbed.
The One who made me laugh,
but not all the time.

Mrs Mermaid

Trouble with little 'un is she's got more hair than head.
He 'ad her, legless,
Flapping up to surface level, tip-toed and out of breath.
Find a nice sea horse, make it easy on yourself,
ah telt her. Lass, dunno what's good for yer.

The tadpole's got less fins than sense.
I know *all* about his kind, hookers for a catch
Them untidy bits hanging out all over,
Pressing and sliding on & off, around gills
where, once, she was streamline, one of us.

Problem with oil spillers is, they spawn all wrong.
That shallow end dip and rub, worse than dolphins.
Try getting him to dance over your seedpods
see where that gets ye, I said.

If he loves you that much lass,
Let 'im come down here.
Let 'im deform himself from the waist down
to prove it.

Who wants to live on land anyway?
If it's so good up there,
Why do airheads come down 'ere, eh?
Nicking coral in fake flippers,
doing it doggy style-less.

Up there, they pick our bones,
hang our inky corpses to sell.
And make us their pets
Merless men babble, unbubbled about the likes of *us*.
Tanked up, they harpoon us double.

They say even maids are dirty.
That girls are sugar and spice, and stink of fish.
Him, with his smoke, and liquor,

and methane, and sweat

Fish only stink when they're dead.

Wake

Watching for clues when to cry,
I count the roses I should have chipped in for.
For the first time, someone says I have a look of her.
As I shuffle dusty moth feet, the docs I should not have worn.
"It's what she would have wanted."

Pouring sherry, and whisky, and laughing after.
Fetta sandwiches, ciabbatta open - on her best china;
passed over from panacklty, dripping on bread.
Endless tea with real milk. Evaporated -
her tinned carnation, cream from a war,
she got a taste for.

This room
never so full since a wedding day,
- Big Jack's christening - her husband's longest nap.
On the Hearth the glass fish is open mouthed
At Visitors, hushed as silver jubilee faces,
in her sacred cabinet.

Later, we clear up soggy napkins, she'd call 'Serviette' -

You wear her gold hoops -

Sulphur air, the slates are wet -
We take bowls from the stereogram -
sip slowly at lime and red pepper soup.

What ever happened to Mary-Mare?

Used to 'ave a right laugh, close as castanets
Me and 'er, till she went all God squad,
Swapped her Levi's for a smock.
"Yer 'avin us on. Good one", I said.
An' she just looked at us, Lady Muck,
like I was a leper. So I waited, like you do,
to gerra few drinks in 'er, get bored sitting in
stroking her belly on a weekend.
But it weren't no phase neither, hung
'er dancin' sandals up for uniform blue.
And *only* blue, when beige was *in*.

She were Chosen, she reckoned, Special.
Didn't look nowt special. *"Mary,
you look like a camel's hump."*
Wiped puke off her chin,
"I'm glowing", she said, *"a vessel."*
"Vessel? Empty headed more like! Whose is it?"
She gawped; cloud up.
like he was Peter Pan or summat.
" There was this angel..."
"Angel? Struth, the earth muster moved!"
Shut 'er gob then, turned 'er face up.
And we stood, mascara to eyelash,
thick as theft.

Last I heard she got hitched, Puppy dog Joe
Always 'ad a thing for 'er.
Snotty knickers, thinks she's better than me.
Went on the lamb when the bailiffs came knocking.
Fat cow on a donkey, done a holy ghost one night,
not even a tara.
What ever 'appened to Mary-Mare?
She used to be me best mate,
Now she calls herself *Virgin*.
Yeah, right.

Romeo's Mistress

Dying that's so sweet,
romantic. If that's your cup
of hemlock, dip a biscuit,
fair enough. Switch off
leave beginnings to imagination.
Make every bloke you meet, ever, a virgin.

But, if you're sore for romancipation,
from a hunk you cannot leave
because he loves you, in his own way,
Listen up sugar, this could be the day.

No matter that Shakey omitted my name,
and gave that other silly wee lassie fame,
made a child martyr manipulated bleedin' heart,
I'm the other woman.
The slapper, bitch.
A mouldy strawberry tart.
I'm the slut, honey,
gonna tear your tragedy apart.

Master Montague's
first was not my last.
His last was not his first.
I rode Romeo.

History's greatest lover?
Give me a break.
Oh Pleaaaase.
Halitosis slurp,
she couldn't even call kiss.
Make no mistake
that Sin on his lips,
was well practised.
Fumbling, on his knees,
squealing sweaty profanities
over a davenport.

Can't say I was surprised
when I heard he'd died:
just that it wasn't sooner.
Any excuse he'd pull that crap with me.
Drown me in reams of soppy poetry.

Pulling his hair, mopping his brow,
clenching fists at stars.
-Oh! Sweet sorrow shining down!
Struth, always something.

Oh Romeo, kid Romeo
Where did your balls go?
This woman doesn't quicken
when you guzzle the perfume on the dresser
each time I leave the room.

Vali Stanley
Modigliani's Women

Vali Stanley was born in
Glasgow in 1958. She has
lived in West Cumbria for
over 20 years and is married
with three daughters
and five terriers.

Morning

She floats an inch above the bed
anchored by his heavy hand.

He is centred, calm and still.
It's like leaning on a breathing log.

He is making her
re-learn herself, inch by inch.

She can tell him anything.
She imagines touching him.

Into his sleeping soul she whispers,
"No-one knows where I am".

What this is

This is a refreshing poem.
Swig it down in one
like a yard of ale.

This is a scary poem.
Read it in the cupboard
underneath the stairs.

This is a trendy poem.
You don't know
What the hell it means.

This is a depressing poem.
I'm too down
to write it.

This is a political poem
Stick it up
all over town.

This poem is a suicide note.
Don't worry
it was quick and painless.

This is a pessimistic poem.
It knows you
won't like it.

This poem is a love letter.
Hide it from
your husband.

Singing Stones

Our worst summer
for sixty years
means little to the pinks
and the pretty salmon
geraniums.

Wind burnt and stunted
in water logged terracotta,
they struggle on.

The sheep marked red this morning
bleed dye into their soggy fleece.
High, bleak, harvested,
the stubbled fields toss
meadowlarks up
like singing stones.

The season brings another chill:
a shadow on the heart.
Tests and
pills in opaque
bottles that he doesn't let
me see him take.

Worry grows here
like grass between flagstones:
deep-rooted,
hard to break.

Meanwhile, the elder ripens
and the brambles stain
our children's fingers
in the narrow, rutted lane.

Extra

I feel like an extra
in the film of your life.
There in the corner,
the one with the quiet face,
trying to catch your attention.

The night when you
re-run it all,
you'll point at me
and say "Who's she?"
Freeze framed, air brushed
and digitally re-mastered,
you won't have the slightest clue
who I was.

Today I'm auditioning for
a speaking part.
Preferably one with gestures,
and a little, subtle
eye contact.

The Catch

The rat's not long dead.
It's a big one:
stretched out straight,
at least a foot.
Its pale grey fur
is soft as a rabbit's.
A gash of scarlet
tags its snout.

Dorian, the tom that caught it,
watches as I pick it up
by the tail, gingerly
between forefinger and thumb,
and stand there
guessing at its weight,
like some seasoned angler
with an early, unexpected trout.

Artist

I want to be that finger on the Sistine
Chapel ceiling, just to have the feeling
I was part of something more.

I'd like to be that sullen girl in front
of Manet's mirror, wearing black velvet
in the Foliés Bergéres.

Or a Degas ballerina with balance
and brio, caught right in the middle
of a perfect entrechat.

A Cézanne apple on white linen.
Any of the women
Modigliani knew.

Vincent Van Gogh's severed ear.

Soft-top

I am the girl
in the red
drop-head sports car.

I make your mouth water.
I wear sunglasses,
and my long hair blows in the wind.

I am the girl
you want to get your hands on,
the one you'd know what to do with.

I am the girl
I am the shiny red lipstick,
you know what I could do with, too.

I am the girl
in the only car you don't mind
overtaking you:"Cop a load of that!"

I am the girl your girlfriend hates.
I am the rich-bitch, man-stealing
cow with a convertible,

and yes, basically,
I want to get
right up your nose.

I want a bumper
sticker that says
"Eat dirt turkeys."

(I'm quite nice actually, I'm somebody's Mrs.)
I'm your fantasy
urban myth.

Perspective

It grows dark about this time
and a red candle burns
beside the dictionary.

I am remembering a kitchen,
yellow curtained,
with apples and parsley
on the table;
the smell of bread;
and laughter there
where Katie, shown perspective,
held trees between her hands.

Love Bites

I want to be where the bad boys are.

Boys with bikes
that are hard
to straddle,
boys with curls
in their upper lip
and scary scars above one eye.

Boys in groups
with cheap guitars,
banging out three
gorgeous chords.
Boys with legs
as long as poles.

Boys who stay awake
for days and come
back driving dodgy cars.
Boys who make
your mother cry.
Boys with names like Raz and Spike.

I want to be where the bad boys are.
I want love bites on my life.

Toadstones

From his winter shelter,
the toad is a watcher.

He reads the plumed
breath of cattle.

His slouching eyes
follow the black-rag

crow's shadow
on the glassy water.

He is older
than this ancient reed bed.

In his head
he grows a stone.

He recognises constellations:
Great Bear, Orion, Pleiades.

He relishes his toady
otherness, his ambiguity,

his place in myth.
His stones lie buried in the earth:

Topaz, emerald, opal, jet.

Lizard

Remember
one day on the high plateau
that was that summer's France,
we walked to Uzés
through the woods above the road?

The heat clung
to our skin
like nylon;
our silences were weighty,
dry as the river bed.

We climbed to where
the bigger houses dazzled;
peeping through hedges
at the watered lush
of gardens and the pools.

Remember
so high there,
the dusty white rock?
(We shared a cigarette,
the smoke tasting like parchment?)

Nearing the town,
you raised a lizard
from the dry grass,
jewel green
and darting.

I remember noticing, quite suddenly
how brown you had become.

Much later, in our cave-cool room,
as water dripped from heavy vines,
Your hands translated me again,
reading my arched, familiar spine
like braille.

Discovery

It wasn't something they'd expected.
Even though they'd all discussed it
in the darker moments at the back
of the drawer beside the bulldog clip.

They'd all had their dreams.

Then a tall stranger came
in a long black coat rifling
through their private pages.
He said, "I'm a poet and I hear
a famous poem lives here."
They said, "Don't be ridiculous."
They said, "Show us some I.D."
But then the short sarcastic
one said, "Sorry boys it's me.
I've been submitting on the side
to little magazines and
independent periodicals."
The poet shook the poem's hand.
"Looks like you've been discovered, mate.
It's time to come with me."

The drawer slid shut with a quiet click.

Later that November night
all their lines pulsed
with possibility.
All their dreaming shone.

Ma

She has a parrot,
and a bog garden
with willow and laburnum.
She grows roses and a rare
blue poppy.

She darns socks,
and turns collars,
makes green tomato
chutney and proper lemonade.

There's always cake in her kitchen,
and the smell of wet dog.
Today, there's sticky chocolate
brownies on the table
and "some ginger things from the W.I."

Her large lap full
of my youngest child
she is prototype granny,
matriarch supreme.

Her presence in our lives
is strong and constant,
unobtrusively there,
like the coins in the hems of our curtains
she sews in to help them fall.

Groupie

I like the drive back,
the road quiet,
the radio playing.

Last time I parked
beside the trees.
I held your book.

And driving on
I felt your words,
burning in my lap.

Proverbs

He was always hot
on proverbs.
I was always shutting
the stable door too late,
putting too many eggs
in my baskets.

He was always keen
on business-speak.
I could never see
the big picture
or the need
for a level playing field.

He was always eager
to find his inner-child.
I had no time
for re-birthing,
being too busy
giving birth.

He was suddenly gone
in a flash of clichéd blonde:
He had to explore his potential.
The children and I
are exploring Peru.
What's meant for you
won't go past you
as he would have said.

Mechanic

I've brought part
of you home
on the roof of my car.

A hand-print
caught complete
in the hard, white frost.

I place my hand
on top of yours.
I watch the edges run.

Detective

How things are put together matters.
I watch the muscle in your upper arm
trace its own importance.
The swell of your breast is a sigh.

I think of being in your house
amongst your things.
Your soft blue shirt.
How much I wanted to look
at what you'd just been writing.

I look for meanings everywhere.
Sometimes everything's a clue.

Today, a cloud above the red
church spire had traced
your shoulder perfectly
against the sky.

Beyond The Pale

I want
to do something irrevocable.
Something I can be held up for.
Something with consequences
too awful to contemplate.

I want
to be caught way out of line.
Well over the limit.
Wearing something far too short
and over the top.

I want
to make your eyes pop out
and your hair turn grey.
I want to make your grandmother
turn cartwheels
in her long-cold grave.

I want
to be the catalyst
for something cataclysmic.
I want to be totally infra dig.
I want to take the biscuit.

Alternatives

If I were a river,
you could slip your bare
brown arms beneath my weeds
and tickle the speckled
brown trout.
Or you could simply lose your footing
and drown in me.

If I were a tree,
You could lie
under my outstretched branches
and see how the sunlight
fingers my leaves.
Or you could simply take a rope
and hang yourself from me.

If I were a flame
I could light your candle.
You could lie
in the dark and use me
to read by.
Or I could simply topple over
and set your bed on fire.

If I were a season,
I'd be spring.
I could come into your garden,
and raise your shoots with my keen hands,
my warming mouth.
Or I could be a late sharp frost,
and with a simple puff of frozen breath,
nip you in the bud.

Baggage

I fold the grey wool cardigan
and put it on top of the suitcase.
It's a mistake to remember everything,
but I'm usually reliable.
Who said what to whom, and where,
and how they looked and if I try really hard,
I'll get the names of the books in the bedroom,
and the name of the scent she was wearing.

See, now I remember her herb garden
through that pergola of Albertine.
The lemon verbena, the borage,
the marjoram, the lovage,
the angelica and the creeping thyme.
See, now I remember planting the spinach
in the plot behind the pink stone wall.
How carefully we nursed those seedlings!
Yet they overshot the mark of fullness,
we gathered only bitter leaves.

I fasten up the zippers and the buckles on the bag,
and carry it downstairs.
The long hall is full of sloping light.
She once said, "Being with you is like trying
to shut a suitcase with too much in it."
These days, I've learnt to say less than I could
and much less than I want to,
and life slips over me like velvet water.

Heather Young
Blocking the Light

Heather Young was born in 1938 into a coal mining family in NW Durham. She began writing poetry after her son died in 1989, aged 24 and her poetry is widely published and anthologised. In 2001 she recieved a Northern Arts award for her prose. She is a member of The Bridge Poets and attends Gillian Allnutt's *Writing from the Inside Out* class and owes inestimable debt to all members for their critical reading of her work. She is currently studying for the MA in Creative Writing at the University of Northumbria.

Acknowledgements
Acknowledgements are due to editors of the following magazines and anthologies: Blue Room Anthology (Diamond Twig Press); Civil Service Author (Winner '97 Comp) ; Lace '95 (Runner-up Comp); Lateral Moves; Never Bury Poetry; Northumbrianna (Comp Winner'97 in dialect form); Other Poetry; Orbis; Poetry Monthly; Tabla (Runner-up Comp); Women's Writers & Journalists (Runner-up Comp'99).

These poems are dedicated to
my parents, who taught me to love books:
my mother, Nora Lawson , née Lambert: 1908-1952
and my father, Edward Gibson Lawson: 1904-1964;

our time was too short

Always

*I'll be loving you, always, with the love that's true, always.
When the things you've planned need a helping hand
I will understand, always. Always...*

My stilettos totter high as the pit shaft
but I'll cope. My mother wore court-shoes:
thicker heels, rounded fronts. More support.

That's when I'll be there, always.

I don't need ecru support bras from The Store -
markets sell my white cotton uplifts
circle stitched for that sweater-girl look.
Black bras are sexy - I could never wear those.
I stick elastoplast on my nipples to stop them
pointing. Ripping it off hurts - it's not fair.

Earrings with screw backs always pinch
dangling over our stove at teatime.
Best is when they caress my cheek as I jive.
Like a kiss. Dancing is awkward in winkle-pickers
but I'll be loving them, wearing them always.
A stab from these Victory-V-sign toes
means business. Mother would laugh. Always.

Modesty dictates a two inch reduction
in the slit of my pencil-slim skirt -
my dimpled knees aren't up to it, as always.
Things might not be fair but my calves
really are shaping up like Betty Grable's.

My mother had smart legs.
When I cried and claimed I looked lumpy
in my school tunic she did agree, cuddled me
assured me puppy fat would not be there always -
would seem like only an hour, or a day
before I would have nothing to fret about.

That Saturday I let the herring burn
as I comforted dad when he needed a helping hand
great tears plopped off his nose onto the hearth.
His Woodbine scattered ash in long fingers
but I didn't chide him.
'Don't worry, Da, it'll be all right. We'll manage.'
That's when I'll be there, always.

'Your mother was a nice lass, pet, and I loved her.'

I went back to the fish, saving them,
scraping black oatmeal onto tatie peelings
already turned red on newspaper.
With the love that's true, always.

That he needed to say it surprised me most.

I hated the hurting. Like a burn. Then he told me
Mary Ellen was coming to live with us. Mary Ellen
with ruby crucifixion earrings and pointy nipples.

Not for just an hour, a day, but always.

Angel Legs

(on visiting Anthony Gormley's 'Angel of the North')

This clinker-coloured knob-head towers
over earth still seamed with coal
as though poking to ignite a spark.

His calves, thighs, buttocks curve
in rugby player's legs
sweeping fast as helter-skelters -
modelled, the sculptor said, on his own

swelling strong like Martin's legs
before chemo ravaged them -
even stripped his feet of flesh
made his sandals slip on and off
plop plop, plop plop, plop plop
like too much rain on his face

splashing onto my face
putting out the spark
pooling in this ground where angels root.

Charity Shop Blouse

Zinging from the 'EVENING WEAR' rail
it glimmers among little black dresses
of 1980s parties. Metallic striped,
a mint humbug in size 12.
Fitting only her reluctant memory…

That Summer she'd worn one the same –
from C & A's sale-rail, then – Sharon
of Queen Vic fame had glittered another
zig-zagging across TVs like a broken dream.
Getting it sorted, though – looking good.

She'd worn hers once: Marbella where sun,
wind, paella, fulfilled every brochure's promise.
Moonglow in her Andalusian waiter's eyes
matched her blouse, her skin. He showed her
where fireflies met the dawn and disappeared.

Now, this confrontation sags, skimpy
on its wire hanger, its power-padded shoulders
limp from too much hot laundering.
Over-priced, out-of-date, the stripes droop
twisted as if blurred by tears.

Hindsight

There's a smugness about hindsight
a clever-clogs told-you-so smirk
like old women over garden walls
arms akimbo - *well fair's fair -
we knew she'd get her fingers burned.*

Whistling out past clenched teeth
pursed lips, tongues clicking fast
as knitting needles, hindsight is powerful:
would have strangled Hitler at birth
saved the Titanic, castrated Henry V111.

Hindsight might have undiscovered tobacco
uninvented the wheel
globally unwarming the Earth
for (even) the underprivileged and poor.
And William Wilberforce? Who was *he?*

Hindsight could have left chemistry
in test tubes nestling in boxes
in Christmas stockings with apples and nuts;
(wondering if stockings that might in time
get holey were such a good idea?)

And apples? Certainly, hindsight might have
proposed a referendum to ban *all* fruit,
especially in public places like Eden.
Or maybe have asked, anyway, what is
this Christmas?

His Wife

comes home tired with antiseptic lingering
smudging bathroom towels, showering down the plug
the stench of urine, illness, death. Earning their mortgage,
the smell of that blunting his appetite for dinner, too.

And let him learn through what kind of stress
she has earned the right to channel-flick
regardless of the European cup. She will remind him
of split shifts, impossible for buying bread and milk

from Asda. Can't he plan the meal? Go shopping after work?
He's got the car weekdays. Well, two weeks out of three.
He'll remind her of traffic jams, road rage, the eighty miles
he travels every day. He's weary, too. Tossing the keys

he misses his target. Unsure what it is.
She heaves to pour herself one glass of Chardonnay
from the bottle brought from France for their Anniversary.
He sidles to the kitchen, bunching over last night's bolognese.

They'll wallow, separate as book-ends, determined
to watch TV shows they'll hardly see.
They'll escape to bed to cling, sleepless on opposing sides.
Tomorrow, not consulting, each calling in for double take-
                                                                    aways.

(with acknowledgement to Ted Hughes' 'Her Husband')

Holiday Snaps

You had a special way of taking photos:
stripped the scene to a skeleton
rebuilt it with, without the viewfinder then
if there was room,
placed me in it where I blended in.

My album: on each page your absences
like a crossword. Those scenes I captured
too lovely to discard - seascapes, mountains
rivers - a hole in each centre with the sun
blazing through where I've cut you out.

Lighting Candles

She's in yet another church:
on holiday - Greek Orthodox this time -
addicted to candlegrease
the glow of firefly flames tapered in rows
slyly winking at her as though they've guessed.

Each visit she lights six candles
any less and who knows what might happen?
Seems an insurance not to huff anyone.
Memory's the thing. Comforting.

There's a knack to conjuring faces
of those who've died; their habits, their smells.
Not by praying, more a concentrated muttering
a shared talking to herself
like a ventriloquist sure of answers.

In Sacre Coeur, once, she even splashed herself
with Holy Water. Not fluttering a signed cross –
more like a sparrow bathing,
anticipating crumbs from a table
scratching at any that may drop.

Lately, when yet another friend dies she wants
to light a bonfire; raging, purifying Hell
singeing ornamental gilt, musty tapestries, icons.
Spewing smoke like a Viking pyre.

She learns how to cope in Bede's St Paul's:
mix her unbelief with local history, beauty, peace,
add a bit of showmanship;
she knows a kind of truce.
Lighting candles seals something. She's not sure what.

Muriel and Me and Roy Rogers

He'd sat beside me when the house was full.
I hadn't noticed as Trigger, panting a fair gallop
chased baddies in black masks.
Roy's horse-whip conjured orchestras
from hills and plains, keeping in pace.
The thump-squeak thump-squeak of our double seats
never missed a beat.
He was panting like he'd joined the chase.

Frozen, I huddled Muriel who cheered
the baddies' capture. One fell off his horse.
Arms raised in surrender, few blows were struck -
the only gunshots meant to warn -
Roy Rogers always fought clean.

His knee did it, sliding from his long coat,
pressing mine. 'Come on, Muriel, get up,
let's sit near the front.'
'What? Never in the dog-end?' she protested.

When the lights went up I squirmed a look
making-on I'd dropped my school beret.
I'd never seen him before: ordinary,
no black mask. I thought I'd made it up.

So, in the second half, lights dimmed
I burned to feel him sneak along our row
passing all those empty seats till *mine*.
The black-and-white screen was a negative,
a shaded still. 'Come on, Muriel, come on - *home.*'
'But we haven't seen the trailer, yet....'

Nearly there, we could run no more.
The sky brimmed blue and birdsong,
again it felt unreal.
Then I saw him, distant,
past the railway yard, gaining fast.
I've never explained why we ran on, exhausted

like all the posses in the West were after us.

And wonder why I felt more threatened
than the baddies.
More ashamed.

Had they not died -

had she bloomed to produce
one bambino after another –
and grown fat, stouter, swollen -
breasts drooping softer than spaghetti
as all good Italian Mommas
were meant to be....
until he turned to another and another
in traditional mode
until their early love grew old....
Best that her immortal words
were heard just once:
>   Wherefore art thou, Romeo?
>   Oh, Romeo, wherefore art thou?

Parcel from Aunt Rose

Crackling brown paper and knotted string
tightly squared in a game of oxo
eight blobs of red wax sealed it, stuck out
like those berries on our Christmas tree
lowered from the loft each December -
this year the parcel was large.

Inside, a note saying they all had colds again
and wasn't the sugar ration paltry?
The usual box of Irish linen handkerchiefs
and a disappointing jigsaw which Dad said
was London Bridge; and a comb, hairbrush
and hand mirror in pale pink celluloid.

In January I practised Principal Girl
After seeing the Empire's Sleeping Beauty panto
then for once I tried the Wicked Queen -
mirror-mirror-on-the-wall pushing plopping
the hand mirror's brittle coating in and out.
It didn't crack until later.

By Summer I'd prop the mirror against
the blue glass candlestick on Grandma's tallboy,
balancing on her bed to view. At school
all the girls had hairs down below, they said.
Had everyone? Even Betty Grable? Even
Princess Elizabeth and Princess Margaret Rose?

Mam kept the paper and string in her handy drawer.
I'd borrow the string for finger games.
Sometimes I played chucks with the wax: they
felt cold as snow, yet not like Christmas at all.
Closed tightly in my palms, they grew hot
and shiny as my new cupid bow lips.

Shopping

Saturday is shopping day,
the day she cuddles images beyond
her butcher's red/white-coated ambiguity
the blur of clean and messy
stirring her in ways she doesn't understand.
Anything special for today, Madam?

Chop-chop-chop has a strength
she's never seen in forty years except
on Channel 4 after Ronald goes to bed.
*Free dripping for the roasting tin? Fat
keeps you warm, Madam. Padding.
Gives you something to get hold of, Madam.*

She has a way with steak & kidney pie.
Onions sliver at her command. Her gravy
thickens with deftness of a wrist twirling
like an unbroken colt. She accepts
the grunting praise, the clean plate:
Saturday is shopping day.

Silent Storms

I struggle not to slip on iced paths.
Snowflakes swirl around the streetlamp
like bees in a hive; the new moon on
bent knee promises more frost.
'Your turn to put the car away.'

Garage door slams shut, shuddering;
back door next: all draughts excluded
by excluder strips, excluding everything.
Locks turn against the storm, confining
central heating closeness.

After cheese sandwiches, trifle, we sit
in stolid TV glare, appositional.
'Forecast's snow,' you announce unnecessarily.
When sleet thrusts crusted panes you ask
'There! Didn't I tell you?'

The washer-dryer turns automatically;
a radiator simmers soap and softener smells
from your socks, my bra to wear tomorrow.
And I still seethe with slights of yesterday,
unresolved and smouldering.

Oblivious, you squint outside, wiping steam
but snow blocks your view: you grunt
'It'll blow over by the morning -
it's far too cold to last.'
'Yes…' I say.

You relish BBC News, football scores,
commentating, not needing assent.
I contemplate past storms, past calms,
my reluctant submission to pattern.
Déjà vu.

Industrious, I unravel wool,
wish I'd hired a video; knitting

young

your next season's cricket sweater,
mentally chest-measuring
without touch.

Sitting Here

He feels awkward sitting here
in this Women's Outpatients' Department
waiting for her to be seen.
How long did they say?

>Stop worrying, you'll be fine -
>in and out in no time at all -
>we were here before that old'un -
>it says complain after twenty minutes
>see - up there?

He's read this Reader's Digest before.
It's like Church the way they whisper
until *her* name then
everybody hears
his wife
has trouble down below.

They're staring at him as though
he has a runny nose.
He might have. You catch
everything going in these places
bugs like Sod's Law - what did she say?
They might want to speak to him?
Ask him,   things?

Him with no ear for women's troubles
the hard clamour of thermometers
the heat on his neck only his own.

Sonnet XV111

(With acknowledgement to the Bard of Avon:
'Shall I compare thee to a Summer's day?'...)

Must she complain each football season long?
He grows more ardent and more dispossessed.
As days grow cold and tighten like a thong
he's on the terrace yelling with the rest.
His uniform is worn with pride, panache:
expensive stripes, unindividual garb.
Not now for him a scarf and anorak,
he swanks in polyester in the bar.
Anxiety will swamp him when they lose;
obsession grip him if by May they win.
All small-talk disappears as Wembley looms –
whole Summer mood depends on 90 mins.

    So long as men can breath or eyes can see,
    so long will goals replay on each TV.

Sunday School

The rumour went around faster
than cartwheels: for reciting your piece
at the Anniversary you'd get a prize,
a book inscribed with your own name.
We all joined.
Practised.

I clutched threepence for each Collection.
Our Corner Shop sold penny-oxos
salty as seaweed
drawing cheeks like bellows –
the cubes were never rationed like sweets.
I always put tuppence on the plate.

Mrs Wilson was sad I had stolen
from less fortunate children
with no ration-coupons at all.
For my own good
she presented my gums
stained like sin

to the whole School,
making me grin
wider than Tarzan's Cheetah.
Worse
I had shopped on The Lord's Day.
The Authorities would be informed.

And the prizes were not
New Adventures Of The Famous Five
but musty as hymnbooks:
Missionaries' Brave Deeds With The Unenlightened,
with very black-and-white illustrations
of unfortunate children.

Swing

Granda made it, chopping redundant rabbit huts
slicing Mam's clothes line. For holes
the poker seared our yard like bonfire night.
Hung between the wall and shrubbery,
croaking like rough-throated frogs, the ropes
shaved themselves. I was a pendulum
beating my songs in a key too high
'Meet me in St Louis, Louis, meet me at the fair.'
When I flew faster, high as the privet
I was Annie on the Deadwood Stage.
Dressing for parts was easy - long frocks, court-shoes
diamante clips, feathered hats. Cupie Doll lips, tasting
scarlet as strawberries, fitted everybody.

I learned the funny feeling
on the upward flight, legs outstretched,
pressing my thighs together, toes grasping
Mam's high-heels tight as the budgie's perch.
My bot squeezed by itself.
- Or was it when I came down?

Once, when I was Carmen Miranda I soared
so high my turban dropped off. I swathed
the curtain-sarong between my legs, catching it
in turn where each hand smoothed the ropes.
By leaning forward and back , the drape
tightened then slackened, tightened, slackened
like making churchbells ring.
It scraped inside my thighs.
It wasn't worth it, wriggling knicker-legs about
to ease elastic nipping inflamed skin.

In the lavvy up the yard my pee stung sharp
as nettles: I bit lips, breaking skin, sucking blood.
Unscrunching newspapers tucked behind pipes
I shook flakes of rust from a torn Picturegoer.
Even without its front page pin-up it was too stiff
for wiping. My knickers were damp all day.

Still Life: Three Apples

(Gallery Offer - £95.00)

Any Teacher would love one,
snacking it, squelched
in a busy Staff Room, ticking
algebra, geography or French verbs.
A sunset in the palm of her hand.

Three blushed orbs in a Universe
of umber clouds; storm-threatened
their light-trapping innocence reflect
1940s schooldays when parcels from abroad
hid jewels smelling of Christmas.

Deep in packing-straw,
Horlicks tablets proved awkward:
scrunched, they coated gums, teeth,
nestled among gaps our Tooth Fairy forgot.
One apple each to make us clean.

The apple I held was a garnet
polished brightest on my pinafore.
I yearned to save it for always,
not knowing then about bruising;
about worms in the core.

I had learned of Eve, though
in Sunday School - imagined Eden's
acres of orchards with branches
to swing on, daring as Tarzan and Jane.
Unaware then, of sweet-talking snakes below.

Turnips

I breathed long grasses,
clutching heaving belly, its stitch
an open wound. The farmer thrashed nearer.
I clasped turnips closer than skin.
No farmer, only Jimmy, scrambling,
skidding stones into the ditch
not meaning to whittle shins.

His chest seeped camphorated oil
consoling as crossed fingers.
Our heartbeats, clamorous as farmer's feet
slowed, synchronised.
'Want some snacker?'
He hacked, scooping slivers from the blade
glistening like his top lip.
'No, I don't like turnip.'

'Then give me a kiss.'
His mouth was a gin trap.
Nostrils whistled louder than wind through corn
front teeth stung like iodine. Lips sucked warm
as Halloween - limp turnip lanterns
fermenting in bins far, far from Postman's Knock.
He allowed air; I stumbled escape.

Other kids there already:
the corrugated iron bus stand saved
from somebody's air-raid shelter
still bent to hide, boomed turnip-stotting.
From the corner the fish-shop's steam cuddled me in.
We shared chips smooth as oysters
sucking salt-and-vinegar drips. Mrs Forster served
Jimmy last: 'I know your game, m'lad.'

Back in the bus stand I jumped highest
easily reaching the roof, springing from the seat
at once a trapeze artist swinging hand-over-hand,
metal-pinging, orchestrating some new beat

unHoly trinity

solo, out of tune;
strangely satisfied, grease-caked lips
holding bitter-sweet tongue.

Blocking the Light

You bend, flash your torch
into my cobwebby cupboard
and I know those buttocks. Vaguely.
'Meterman!' you'd called. No clues
bar your height - that's about right -
and your stride; the haunch
of your shoulders as you leave?

Yesterday's lover. Were you ever?
Paunchy, with Bobby Charlton hairstyle -
but that sideways smile, like an apology -
the same? No reason to suppose you knew me,
my new size twenty spread blocking the light.
But did you ever really read my mind?
Meet my every need?

I let my belly back out, ballooning,
miserable as I stroke my jowels folding
like Nora Batty tights.
I have the urge to shoot you dead,
meter-reading messenger; but
console myself that
you must be your father.

Why not keep bang up to date with IRON developments?
Our web site contains news, links to
other publishing sites, future plans
and much more.
www.ironpress.co.uk

Poetry Cards

One of these unique poetry cards
- suitable for every occasion -
comes free with every book. The poems are:
Cullercoats, by **Mike Wilkin** &
Tynemouth, by **Kitty Fitzgerald**.
Please state preferences
when ordering.

COMING SOON
from IRON Press

THE SINGING MEN
A collection of short stories by Derek Gregory

MARMALADE SEASON
A new collection of poetry by Katie Campbell